Gaming Unchained

The Influence of Blockchain on the Video Game Industry

Table of Contents

Chapter 1. Introduction

In this Special Report, we delve into the fascinating frontier of "Gaming Unchained: The Influence of Blockchain on the Video Game Industry". As you turn the pages, you'll uncover the new horizon of video gaming that marries cutting-edge blockchain technology with innovative gameplay. Don't worry if you're not a tech wizard; our report simplifies the complex dynamics of blockchain in an everyday language that both gamers and non-gamers will effortlessly grasp. Within these pages, we unravel the transformative impact of blockchain on the gaming landscape, its possibilities, challenges, and the exciting future it promises. So brace yourself for an engrossing journey - because videogaming as you know it, is about to get a blockchain-powered revamp! Unearth this enriching knowledge with us, and you'll never see gaming - or blockchain - in quite the same light again.

Chapter 2. Understanding the Basics: Video Games and Blockchain Technology

Blockchain technology and video games are two concepts that many people wouldn't naturally associate with each other. But when you peel back the layers, you can see that they're actually a perfect match. Blockchain technology provides a secure, transparent platform for transactions and records. Video games, on the other hand, are inherently virtual and digital, and have a history of pioneering new technological advancements. In this chapter, we will explore these two realms, understanding the basics of both video games and blockchain technology.

2.1. Blockchain Basics

Blockchain technology is essentially a vast, global distributed ledger or database running on millions of devices and open to anyone, where not just information but anything of value - money, votes, music, art, intellectual property, even an in-game item - can be moved, stored and managed securely and privately. It functions as a decentralized system, where no single entity or group has control, but control is distributed across the network where each participant has access to a secure, immutable record of data.

At the heart of a blockchain is a protocol that validates, records, and replicates data across multiple nodes, ensuring that it cannot be altered or deleted. Each set of transactions creates a new 'block' which is added to the 'chain' of previous transactions, thus forming a 'blockchain'. This transparency, decentralization and security make blockchain a revolutionary technology.

One of the key byproducts of the advent of blockchain technology is cryptocurrencies, of which Bitcoin is the most well-known. Decentralized finance, NFT (Non-fungible token), supply chain management, and of course, gaming, are some of the areas where blockchain has started showing its influence.

2.2. The World of Video Games

Video games have become a dominant player in the entertainment industry. They have evolved significantly, from the simple pixelated graphics games of the early days to the multiplayer online games of today with breathtaking graphics. We've traveled a long journey from Pong to immersive experiences provided by games like World of Warcraft or The Elder Scrolls.

Video games create virtual environments that enable players to interact with visual interfaces. Unlike traditional games, video games combine sound, dynamic visuals and storytelling to immerse the player in a unique interactive experience. There are different game genres, each with their own unique gameplay, including role-playing games (RPG), first-person shooter (FPS), real-time strategy (RTS), massively multiplayer online role-playing games (MMORPG), and many more.

The gaming industry is continuously expanding, reaching a broader audience, thanks to the rise of mobile gaming and esports. Tech developments like virtual reality, augmented reality, game streaming, and cloud gaming are signaling the next revolution in the industry.

2.3. Where Gaming Meets Blockchain

As video games and blockchain technology are both digital and involve complex computing, it is only natural that some would endeavor to integrate the two, leveraging the best of each to create a superior product. The realm where these two overlap is commonly known as blockchain gaming.

Combining video games with blockchain technology could lead to a number of new and exciting opportunities. The security advantages of blockchain could help address fraud issues in video games. It could fundamentally change the outlook of in-game economies. With blockchain, all in-game transactions would be transparent and verified. Therefore, it wouldn't just create a space for developers and gamers, but also for collectors, traders, and investors.

In a blockchain-based game, every item could be tokenized and owned by a player on the blockchain, creating an economy of unique items. This concept has been used in games like CryptoKitties and Decentraland. An open, collaborative gaming environment can be created where assets can be traded across different games, encouraging interoperability - a concept unthinkable in traditional video games.

2.4. The Potential Challenges

Despite the potential, the integration of blockchain and video gaming is not without its challenges. One of the obstacles includes scalability issues since blockchain networks have a limit on the number of transactions they can handle per second. In a video game where countless interactions are happening every second, this could pose a problem.

Another issue is accessibility. While blockchain usage is growing, it's still a complex technology for many to grasp, potentially adding a barrier to entry for some gamers. Also, the perceived anonymity and lack of regulation of blockchain might discourage mainstream adoption.

Moreover, there are legal and regulatory challenges. The classification of blockchain game tokens (whether as cryptocurrencies, securities, commodities or something else) is an open question, which can lead to unexpected legal complications for both developers and players.

2.5. Looking Forward: A Blockchain-Powered Gaming Future

There is no doubt that blockchain technology holds great promise for the gaming industry. It could offer a level of interaction, ownership, and transparency that has been unheard of in traditional video games. Despite the challenges, many believe these can be addressed as the technology matures and as standards, norms, and regulations evolve.

As we move forward, we can expect to see more games that make use of blockchain technology. We might soon witness a gaming world where every item, every character, and every environment is tokenized on the blockchain.+

Chapter 3. The Evolution of Blockchain in Gaming

The evolution of blockchain in video games has been as dynamic and rapidly changing as the technology itself. From small beginnings, it has grown into a significant trend that has greatly influenced the game development industry. Blockchain technology, in essence, allows for the creation of decentralized digital ledgers that provide secured, transparent, and pseudonymous record-keeping.

3.1. The Beginning: Blockchain's Entry Into Gaming

When blockchain technology initially infiltrated the gaming industry, it targeted the in-game assets field. CryptoKitties, a game developed by Axiom Zen in 2017, is often credited as the first major implementation of blockchain in a gaming context. Through the use of blockchain, CryptoKitties allowed players to breed, purchase, and sell virtual cats, with each cat being a non-fungible token (NFT) stored on the blockchain.

3.2. Digital Assets and Ownership

With the introduction of CryptoKitties, blockchain's potential to revolutionize in-game assets started to draw interest. Before the advent of blockchain, digital assets in video games were owned by the game developers, not the players. With blockchain, however, virtual goods became assets that could be owned, traded, and sold by players outside of the game's universe. These individual assets exist on the blockchain, independent of the game, and cannot be altered by anyone, including game developers or other players.

For example, think of a rare weapon you've acquired in a game. Today, this weapon has little or no value outside of the game environment. But in blockchain-integrated games, the weapon becomes a digital asset that can be traded or sold on various platforms. These assets acquire real-world monetary value, blurring boundaries between virtual and real economies.

3.3. Blockchain in Mainstream Gaming

As the potential of blockchain to revolutionize gaming came to light, several major players in the gaming industry started to take notice. Ubisoft, a gaming giant, has been exploring blockchain technology since 2018 through its Strategic Innovation Lab, which studies emerging technologies and their applicable use cases.

In 2019, Ubisoft became a block producer for an experimental project called "Ultra," designed to test the scalability of blockchain in gaming. Ubisoft's interest in blockchain represents a significant step toward mainstream adoption and heralds the potential of blockchain's future in gaming.

3.4. Integration of Cryptocurrencies into Gaming

So far, the use of cryptocurrencies in gaming has been relatively limited, restricted primarily to the trading of in-game assets. However, blockchain technology opens the doors to wider use possibilities, such as integrating a game's internal economies with cryptocurrencies.

Imagine being able to earn cryptocurrency through in-game actions or achievements, and then being able to spend that currency either within the game, or in the real world. This bridging of the gap between gaming and real-world economies can significantly transform the player engagement and monetization dynamics.

These innovations are only beginning to surface, with games like "Lightnite," a battle-royale game that integrates Bitcoin rewards in its gameplay, leading the charge.

3.5. The Future of Blockchain in Gaming

While the journey of blockchain's introduction into gaming has been exciting so far, the technology's true potential in this field remains largely untapped. One frontier that is beginning to get explored is the use of blockchain for game integrity and fairness.

In competitive gaming or esports, cheating and unfair practices can cast a shadow over the game's integrity. Blockchain, with its immutable and transparent nature, can provide solutions to these challenges, recording game results in a way that cannot be altered or manipulated. This could safeguard the spirit of fair competition, making games more enjoyable and reliable for players.

In addition, blockchain's application in decentralized gaming platforms can disrupt traditional distribution channels. The current gaming industry is dominated by large corporations that control the distribution of games. Blockchain could democratize this process, making crowdfunding and independent distribution easier and more accessible for smaller game developers.

Thus, the journey of blockchain in the world of video games is just starting. Along the challenging, thrilling path ahead, it promises to reshape the gaming landscape, offering new avenues of immersion, monetization, and fair play. Time will tell what the widespread embracing of blockchain will mean for the future of the gaming industry, but for now, the possibilities seem exciting, endless, and full of potential.

Chapter 4. Revolutionizing Gaming Economics: Cryptocurrencies and Tokens

Any journey into the world of video gaming economics begins with credits, coins, or tokens – the lifeblood of a vast majority of games, which enable players to access resources, levels, and characters.

4.1. Evolving from In-Game Currencies

Historically, virtual currencies have been confined to their respective game universes. They've empowered gamers to buy virtual goods and services within a specific game but have little to no value in the outside world. This virtual game economy has traditionally been a rather closed system.

From the earliest incarnations of 'Pac-Man' where accumulating points was the sole objective, to modern MMORPGs (Massively Multiplayer Online Role-Playing Games) like 'World of Warcraft' in which in-game gold facilitates trade, we've seen the interplay of supply, demand, and digital currencies forming game economies.

4.2. Blockchain Ushers a New Era

However, the advent of blockchain technology and the associated rise of cryptocurrencies is exciting because it drastically reimagines this concept. With the blockchain ledger's decentralized and immutable nature, virtual assets - whether currencies or other game collectibles - can be assigned real-world value and exchanged across game boundaries.

By blending in-game assets with blockchain, we can redefine existing economics, enable unprecedented player ownership, and create new monetization strategies for game developers.

4.3. The Dawn of Player Ownership

The potential of player ownership is a significant shift from traditional gaming economics. In previous models, once a player had purchased an in-game currency or item, the item remained under the game's control. Players could use them only in ways pre-defined by the game developers, often losing access if the game was discontinued.

Blockchain changes this paradigm by offering players "true ownership" of their virtual assets. By tokenizing in-game assets via blockchain, developers can grant players the ability to trade, sell, or keep these assets as an investment. Assets become Non-Fungible Tokens (NFTs), each holding unique attributes, which further enhances the value and uniqueness of the gaming items.

4.4. Cryptocurrencies - The New In-Game Gold

Cryptocurrencies such as Bitcoin and Ethereum are becoming increasingly accepted in the gaming industry. They aren't just allowing players to buy assets within games directly, but the line between in-game currencies and real-world money is blurring.

Cryptocurrencies provide a universal format for in-game transactions, solving the challenges of converting one game's currency into another, all while reducing transaction costs. They are interoperable, allowing players to carry value across games.

They also add a layer of security, thanks to the inherent characteristics of blockchain technology - immutability, transparency, and security. As gaming becomes more competitive, these features will ensure fair, cheat-proof gaming tied to indisputable payments and rewards.

4.5. Encouraging Player Investment

With the rise of player ownership and acceptance of real-world value cryptocurrencies, games emerge as a new investment avenue. Gamers are no longer consumers but shareholders who can benefit from the game's success.

Consider 'CryptoKitties', a pioneer in this space - a blockchain-based virtual game that allows players to purchase, collect, breed and sell various types of virtual cats, with each cat being a unique NFT. In 2017, a "CryptoKitty" was reportedly sold for $170,000. This introduces another element into the gaming industry – speculation.

4.6. Challenges and Considerations

Not all everything is smooth sailing, though. This new gaming economy landscape brings with it a multitude of challenges. The volatility of cryptocurrencies is a concern, with the value of virtual assets fluctuating dramatically. Legal frameworks in many countries have not caught up with this new reality, making regulation murky. Leveling the playing field for players with varying investment abilities could become a hurdle.

4.7. The Shape of Things to Come

However, these challenges are expectantly solvable as the technology matures and legal systems adapt. An ecosystem of different games interconnected by shared blockchain-based economies might not be far off. Developers can devise new gameplay mechanics around the player-driven economy. Consumer interest, driven by the possibility of tangible profits, is likely to skyrocket.

In essence, blockchain-based game economies have the potential to revolutionize how we play games, think of 'value' in games, and even how we perceive the divide between the 'virtual' and the 'real' world.

Video games economies, as we know them, are changing. Armed with blockchain technology, cryptocurrencies, and tokens, developers and players alike stand to gain. These elements push the boundaries of interactivity, engagement, and monetization, promising a future for video games that's as exciting as it is revolutionary.

Chapter 5. Smart Contracts: The Bedrock of Trust and Transparency in Games

The bedrock of blockchain technology and its integration into any industry - including gaming - centers around an innovative concept known as 'smart contracts'. In their simplest form, smart contracts refer to self-executing agreements with the terms directly written into code. They automatically perform transactions and other actions when conditions set out in the contract are met.

5.1. Understanding Smart Contracts

A smart contract is digital, decentralised, and public – it lives on the blockchain where everyone on the network can see it. But its content is secure, and any changes to it require collective approval. Think of a smart contract as a vending machine – you place a token, the machine recognizes it, and then releases the product.

The power of smart contracts lies in their ability to do away with intermediaries. Because they're programmable, they can execute when specified conditions are met, making operations more efficient, transparent and cost-effective.

Where does this figure in gaming? We'll explore this extensively as we journey into scenarios where smart contracts have been woven into the fabric of games.

5.2. Smart Contracts in Games: Suitability and Enhancements

From purchasing weapons to trading unique gaming items, the gaming industry has become a complex economy in its own right. Enter the 'smart contracts' - they can automate in-game transactions, verify ownership of virtual assets, and maintain player data in a transparent, tamper-proof manner.

Multiplayer online games involve extensive trading of in-game resources. Ensuring this process goes smoothly, is fair, and can't be exploited is a significant challenge. However, smart contracts can be programmed to handle such transactions automatically – ensuring trust that is crucial in such trades.

Micropayments for incremental content are a feature in many online games. Rather than using credit cards (inviting concerns over security and transaction fees), players can personally transact using cryptocurrencies. This format supported by blockchain's smart contracts adds a layer of trust and transparency that is absent in current centralized systems.

5.3. The Potential of Tokenization

Utilizing blockchain's smart contracts, gaming properties can be tokenized into unique, non-fungible tokens (NFTs). These tokens represent ownership of a digital item, character, or other game resources, offering the player full control over their virtual assets.

Gamers can own, trade, or sell these NFT assets in the public market, driving a new revenue stream. Furthermore, unlike traditional markets, transactions are secure, transparent, cheaper and faster thanks to the integrity of blockchain and smart contracts.

The tokenization of in-game assets could be a game-changer in the industry, offering a novel method for gamers to truly own the fruits of their gameplay.

5.4. Challenges and Considerations

While smart contracts in games offer an exciting new frontier of possibilities, they also come with challenges. The primary concern involves regulatory issues, as transactional laws vary vastly across geographic regions. Further, there's a need to educate users about the technology to foster adoption.

It is vital to ensure the security of these smart contracts. Any vulnerability could lead to theft or loss of players' digital property. Therefore, implementing blockchain and smart contracts requires robust security measures to protect users' digital assets.

Another consideration that cannot be overlooked is the scalability issue. As increasing number of transactions occur in the system, the technology should be capable enough to handle the load without disruption.

5.5. Setting The Stage for a Blockchain-powered Future

Blockchain's integration with video gaming, driven in large part by smart contracts, is still in the early stages. But the transformation it promises to bring about, from nurturing a robust virtual economy to safeguarding player immersion, is exhilarating.

In this 'unchained' gaming world, smart contracts lay the foundation for a more engaging, transparent, and user-centric gaming experience. It pushes the envelope, allowing the sector to cater to the evolving demands of gamers who seek more agency and ownership. The challenges it brings about are indeed critical hurdles. But given the transformative potential of this technology, the journey to overcome these challenges can certainly lead us into a new era of gaming – one that is more dynamic, fair and secure than ever before.

The future is brimming with potential. And as every player would know, no game worth playing is ever won without overcoming a few critical challenges. Here's to the future of gaming – may it be as vibrant, challenging, and engrossing as the games that fuel our passion.

As developers and players begin to explore the potential of smart contracts and blockchain in gaming, there's a promise of revolution - where games are developed not just for gamers, but by gamers themselves – a promise of an inclusive, participative, and unchained gaming future. With blockchain technology, the game truly never stops!

Chapter 6. Cryptokitties and Beyond: The Phenomenon of Blockchain Games

In late 2017, a curious phenomenon arose within the nascent intersection of blockchain and gaming: Cryptokitties. This game, which allowed users to breed, collect, and sell digital cats, dominated headlines and brought the concept of blockchain gaming into popular consciousness for the first time. A seemingly whimsical concept, Cryptokitties nonetheless marked a sea-change moment in the gaming industry - and beyond.

6.1. The Emergence of Cryptokitties

Cryptokitties was developed by Axiom Zen and launched in November 2017. Players could buy, sell, and mate virtual cats – each represented as an ERC721 non-fungible token (NFT) on the Ethereum blockchain. The term 'non-fungible' means that each kitty was unique, with its own set of characteristics defined by smart contracts.

The success of Cryptokitties was nothing short of meteoric. In less than a week, transactions relating to the game had become so numerous that they took up nearly 25% of Ethereum's entire processing capacity. By December, players had reportedly spent over $6.7 million buying and breeding these digital pets. Rare kitties went for incredibly high stakes, with the most expensive one sold at the time, 'Dragon', priced at 600 ETH, equivalent to around $170,000.

6.2. Understanding the Appeal

Cryptokitties' charm lies not only in its playful premise but also in its groundbreaking utilization of blockchain technology. The game introduced the concept of "true ownership", which meant that players had full control over their digital assets and could freely trade them. Unlike conventional games where assets remain under the control of the gaming company, Cryptokitties allowed users to own their kitties unequivocally as these assets were secured in their blockchain addresses.

Also, the game incorporated the concept of 'provable scarcity', meaning the maximum number of kitties that could ever exist was predefined in the smart contract. Thus making even the common kitties valuable due to their finite number. These game mechanics were revolutionary at the time and play a large part in explaining Cryptokitties' explosive popularity.

6.3. Limitations and Implications

Despite its resounding success, Cryptokitties wasn't without flaws. The game's popularity highlighted the scalability issues of the Ethereum blockchain, as the sudden influx of transactions significantly slowed down the network. This led to an increase in the gas prices (transaction fees on Ethereum), making the game expensive to play.

The Cryptokitties phenomenon also sparked some criticisms. Many saw it as an embodiment of the irrational exuberance surrounding cryptocurrencies and blockchain technologies at the time. As prices for rare kitties soared, critics perceived the game as a sort of digital Beanie Baby bubble.

Yet, at the same time, Cryptokitties' success showed the potential and promise of blockchain-enabled gaming. It swiftly demonstrated how blockchain technology could revolutionize the gaming industry by enabling the tokenization of in-game assets, providing true ownership, allowing peer-to-peer transactions, and creating provable scarcity.

6.4. The Influence on Blockchain Gaming

In its wake, Cryptokitties left a considerable impact on the broader blockchain gaming landscape. The game's success inspired a myriad of other blockchain-based games involving the tokenization of in-game assets. Notable examples include Gods Unchained, Axie Infinity, and Decentraland.

Gods Unchained, for instance, is a digital card game where players own their cards as NFTs. In a similar vein, Axie Infinity allows players to breed, raise, and battle fantasy creatures named Axies, while Decentraland is a virtual reality platform powered by the Ethereum blockchain, where users can create, experience, and monetize content and applications.

More recently, blockchain gaming has entered the realm of eSports, with projects like ChiliZ providing blockchain-based solutions to enhance fan engagement. In these systems, fans can purchase tokens linked to their favourite eSports teams, providing them a say in team decisions and access to exclusive content.

6.5. The Future Beyond Cryptokitties

Looking ahead, the potential of blockchain in gaming stretches far beyond digital kitties and eSports tokens. Concepts like decentralized gaming, play-to-earn, and blockchain-based virtual economies are gaining traction. With developments like the user-owned virtual world of Somnium Space, the ecosystem-service game Alien Worlds, and the DeFi-oriented farmer's game Yield Guild, the boundaries of what constitutes a 'blockchain game' are continually expanding.

The future promises a gaming world where players have real,

tangible stakes in the games they play, from owning and selling in-game assets to influencing game development decisions. With these new developments, the question is no longer if, but how, blockchain technology will shape the future of the gaming industry. In the long view, Cryptokitties was merely the first step in an extended journey - a fascinating adventure across the uncharted terrain of blockchain gaming.

In this rapidly evolving landscape, the gaming industry is poised to undergo a radical transformation, driven by blockchain technology. The phenomenon that started with Cryptokitties has moved past being just a curiosity. It has unveiled unprecedented possibilities for enhancing gameplay and deepening player engagement. As the convergence of gaming and blockchain continues to unfold, players, developers, and investors alike are set for an thrilling ride into the future of gaming. The era of blockchain gaming is just beginning. Expect the unexpected, because the games you play - and how you play them - are about to radically change.

Chapter 7. Decentralized Gaming Spaces: Emergence of Virtual Worlds

Decentralized gaming spaces, a groundbreaking innovation brought forth by the blockchain revolution, are fundamentally reshaping the way we explore, interact with, and own elements within virtual worlds. They are bringing about novel levels of flexibility and user autonomy, freedom and interaction, as well as a sense of ownership that could only be dreamt about before.

7.1. Emergence of Blockchain in Gaming

The genesis of leveraging blockchain technology in video games traces its roots back to 2014, with the emergence of "HunterCoin". A modest yet pioneering endeavour, this game employed blockchain as a fundamental part of its gameplay, allowing players to mine the cryptocurrency by playing the game itself.

However, blockchain's real breakout moment in the gaming industry came in the shape of CryptoKitties in 2017. The game, which allows players to purchase, collect, breed, and even sell virtual cats on the Ethereum network, skyrocketed in popularity and demonstrated the untapped potential of gaming on the blockchain. From this moment, it became emphatically clear that blockchain technology could bring unprecedented changes to the world of gaming and significantly enhance the way players interact with in-game assets.

Decentralized gaming spaces have blossomed from this vision, enabling the possession of in-game items, real-estate, and other virtual assets on a decentralized blockchain network - an ownership that is verifiable, indelible and transparent.

7.2. Why Decentralized Spaces?

With the advent of blockchain, players can now take 'ownership' to a whole new level. This technology grants users the power to truly own in-game assets in the form of non-fungible tokens (NFTs), transforming them from temporary digital assets into unique, tradable commodities.

These NFTs, governed by smart contracts, allow players to buy, trade, sell, or even loan their assets on different blockchain-powered platforms, overriding the limitations posed by traditional gaming systems. Additionally, this new era of "Playable NFTs" is creating endless opportunities for game developers to think out-of-the-box and deliver unparalleled gaming experiences.

Moreover, blockchain's inherent transparency and verifiability give players total visibility of all their transactions. Players can look up the history, quality, and real value of their digital commodity any time they wish to.

This true sense of digital ownership is undeniably a boon for avid gamers. But apart from enhanced ownership, on blockchain-governed games, players also get to engage within a provably fair system; one where the rules are immutable, and the outcomes, determined by transparent computation, rather than a centralized server's hidden mechanics.

7.3. Popular Platforms and Games

Today, an array of decentralized gaming spaces exist, each with its unique blend of concepts, platforms, and ecosystems:

1. Decentraland: One of the pioneers, Decentraland is an Ethereum-

based virtual reality platform. It allows users to purchase land via the NFT marketplace, and on these lands, they can freely build, create experiences, and monetize them to other users.

2. CryptoVoxels: An Ethereum-based virtual world, CryptoVoxels enables players to build, develop and sell property. It blends aspects of social interaction, gaming, and e-commerce onto a digital realm, as enthusiasts purchase plots of virtual land to erect their unique structures.

3. Somnium Space: An immersive blockchain-backed VR world, where players can own, develop and trade pieces of land, assets, avatars, or experiences. Thanks to its integration with the Ethereum network, the virtual land within Somnium Space holds real-world value, paving a unique path for gamers, creators, and entrepreneurs.

4. Axie Infinity: This game has introduced a novel gameplay model, often referred to as 'Play to Earn'. Players can collect, breed, battle, and trade fantastical creatures known as Axies. These creatures are NFTs and thus have real market value, making the game remarkably profitable for some of its players.

7.4. The Challenges Ahead

While decentralized gaming worlds are an intriguing growth story, this progress also comes with its share of hurdles.

Mass adoption is a significant concern. While the concept of true digital ownership and play-to-earn mechanics is exciting for existing stakeholders of the blockchain space, the average gamer remains largely unaware or skeptical of these opportunities. Bridging this gap remains a hefty task for the industry.

Security remains another crucial issue, given the real-world value associated with these assets. Ensuring the safety of blockchain-based games and platforms against hacking or fraud attempts requires strong security measures and extensive education for players, about safe practices while interacting with these platforms.

Finally, the questions on regulation and legalities. Since the landscape of blockchain and cryptocurrency remains a patchwork of different laws across the world, defining clear rules for these decentralized spaces can be a tricky affair.

7.5. Conclusion: A Brave - and Decentralized - New World

Regardless of the challenges, the decentralized gaming space continues to burgeon, and its impact on gaming economics and paradigms can't be overstated. As we move forward, gaming developers and designers are learning to strike a better balance between the technicalities of blockchain and the immersive, fun element that gaming has always been about.

Emerging trends like Metaverse, a collective virtual shared space that's continuously evolving, and NFTs becoming integral parts of gameplay, herald an exciting era for both the gaming and the blockchain industry.

Change is inevitable, and gaming - as we used to know it - is undeniably changing. It's making a shift from being a realm of make-believe endeavors to a tangible world where virtual assets are as real as home, possessions, and money in the physical space. The future of gaming lies not in closed, compartmentalized worlds operating on centralized servers, but in transparent, open, and truly global landscapes powered by decentralization.

Chapter 8. The Challenges of Integrating Blockchain into Gaming

Integrating blockchain into the video game industry presents incredible opportunities, but it's not without its challenges. As we embark on this exploration of hurdles that developers and companies face, remember that every technological leap carries its share of difficulties that must be faced head-on.

8.1. Technological Challenges

One of the most fundamental obstacles lies in the overall complexity of the blockchain technology itself. Even though video game developers are familiar with complex coding systems and architecture, blockchain, with its cryptographic algorithms and consensus protocols, is a whole new beast to tackle.

Achieving a balance between decentralization (a core tenet of blockchain) and ensuring a smooth gameplay experience is another challenge. Traditional games rely on centralized servers that ensure latency is kept to a minimum, ensuring seamless in-game performance. With blockchain, every action has to be confirmed by the network, which could lead to lag if not properly optimized.

Security also poses significant challenges. While the blockchain ecosystem is hailed for its security features, it opens new security threat vectors too. Securely storing cryptocurrency assets with robust security mechanisms is necessary to prevent potential cyber-attacks.

8.2. Regulatory and Legal Challenges

The legal and regulatory landscape that surrounds blockchain is still in a flux. The public decentralization nature of blockchain and the use of cryptocurrency in gaming can attract regulatory attention. Developers must be wary of implications around anti-money laundering laws, data protection, and tax liabilities.

In many regions, virtual assets and tokens are still not recognized legally. The sale and purchase of in-game assets using cryptocurrency could technically qualify as a transaction that should be taxed, though how laws will ultimately be applied in this space remains unclear. Game developers will need to navigate these ambiguities.

8.3. Economic Challenges

Establishing a fair, balanced in-game economy is a significant challenge in itself. If players can trade assets freely, prices can fluctuate dramatically due to supply and demand, potentially disrupting gameplay and causing balance issues.

Moreover, scalability issues with blockchains can limit the number of transactions per second (TPS), making it harder to handle microtransactions, a significant part of many gaming economies. Solutions such as Layer 2 protocols are in development, but they need to mature.

8.4. Societal Challenges

A shift to blockchain-based gaming also brings cultural and societal challenges. The stigma around cryptocurrencies, often associated with illegal activities, might deter some communities from participating. Educating players not only about the gaming experience but also about asset management and security will be crucial.

8.5. Development and Adoption Challenges

For developers, the learning curve associated with understanding and working with blockchain can be steep. It's not just about integrating a new technology; it's about reconceiving game design principles.

The uncertainty also extends to the end users—the players. Even expert players might be hesitant to embrace a system they're not familiar with. Overcoming user resistance, and getting gamers to understand, trust, and adopt blockchain gaming, can be a challenge in itself.

8.6. Tackling the Challenges

While the challenges are multi-faceted, they are not insurmountable. Mitigation begins with understanding the technology itself, its limitations, and its potential.

Blockchain development for gaming would require specialized skill sets. A robust, engaging gaming experience needs to be coupled with a secure and viable asset management system.

Forming partnerships can be beneficial. Traditional gaming companies and blockchain companies could collaborate to share knowledge, understand challenges, and create solutions.

For a smoother adoption, a phased approach may be a suitable solution. Instead of an abrupt blockchain switch, games could integrate certain features in stages, allowing players to ease into the system incrementally.

Regulators and developers must seek common ground. Compliance with regulations shouldn't stifle innovation. Learning from past blockchain mistakes can help shape an amicable regulatory framework that promotes advancement and ensures player protection.

8.7. The Road Ahead

It's exciting—but also a bit daunting—to consider how blockchain could revolutionize the gaming industry. The challenges are substantial, but they are also an opportunity to create a more rewarding, immersive gaming experience for players globally. As we forge ahead with blockchain in gaming, it's uplifting to envisage a future where players have true ownership over their in-game assets, where creators are fairly rewarded for their innovations, and where blockchain becomes an integral part of the gaming tapestry.

Chapter 9. Championing Player Ownership: Real-world Value in Virtual Assets

Imagine residing in a world where the lines between reality and virtuality are blurred, where the fruits of your digital grind can very well translate into a tangible advantage in your real life. Now, that's not a concept out of a William Gibson's cyberpunk, but a very real possibility unfolding with the amalgamation of blockchain technology and video gaming. This chapter aims to dissect that possibility, primarily focusing on how blockchain champions player ownership by providing real-world value to virtual assets.

9.1. The Concept of Virtual Assets

Ever since video gaming stepped out of the arcades and found its way into personal computers and consoles, the concept of virtual assets has come to the forefront. These assets, anything from characters, skins, weapons, or power-ups to in-game currency, play a crucial role in enriching the gaming experience. Traditionally, players could earn these assets by progressing through levels or, in some cases, through in-app purchases.

However, the classic gaming set-up has always treated these digital assets with an air of ephemerality. They existed in the enclosed servers of gaming companies and had no value outside the gaming universe. Although your avatar might be wielding a legendary sword in the virtual world, in the real world, it held no value. This lack of permanence and ownership is where gaming met its limits - limits that blockchain technology is gearing up to transcend.

9.2. The Blockchain Advantage

As much as blockchain technology is about security and decentralization, it's also about ownership. Blockchain revolutionizes the concept of virtual assets by offering them permanence and interoperability, thus creating an entirely new economy of digital goods.

The backbone of this revolution is a class of tokens known as Non-Fungible Tokens (NFTs), unique digital assets associated with distinctive attributes and secured on a blockchain. Unlike cryptocurrencies such as Bitcoin or Ether, where each unit holds the same value, no two NFTs are alike due to their individual metadata. Such an attribute makes them represent unique ownership over digital goods and assets.

Virtual assets backed by NFTs live on a decentralized system. They are no longer confined within the periphery of a single game developed by a game studio but can exist independently on a public ledger. This permanence allows one to trade these virtual items freely within and outside the gaming ecosystem, providing them with real-world market value.

9.3. Trading Virtual for Real: Unveiling the Marketplace

The decentralization of virtual assets offers birth to an exciting marketplace that works parallel to the real-world economy. Players can now own, sell, buy, or even rent their digital assets through various blockchain-based platforms like OpenSea, Rarible, and Axie Marketplace.

Imagine if the rare weapon skin you scored in a game could be sold for real-world money in a peer-to-peer marketplace, or the virtual land you claimed in a metaverse (think Decentraland) forms an excellent digital estate investment. Blockchain is bridging this gap, allowing gamers to realize the value of their time and effort invested in accumulating these virtual assets.

Here's where smart contracts come into play. These are programmatically designed contracts that operate on the blockchain, enabling the trustless trade of assets. It means that on successful completion of the transaction, the smart contract ensures mutual exchange of assets without the need for an intermediary, further strengthening the paradigm shift towards a decentralized gaming economy.

9.4. Challenges Along the Blockchain Highway

Despite its alluring charm, blockchain integration in gaming is not without hurdles. The most significant challenge comes from scalability issues. Current public blockchain networks can handle only a limited number of transactions per second, a constraint when considering the high velocity and volume of transactions in the gaming industry.

Moreover, the steep learning curve and the need for players to have a basic understanding of blockchain and cryptocurrencies could deter many from embracing this technology. Additionally, the volatility of the cryptocurrency market adds a layer of unpredictability that could affect the value of a player's virtual assets.

9.5. Glimpsing Into the Blockchain-Enriched Future

The narrative of video gaming is being rewritten with each line of blockchain code. And although still in its nascent stage, it is gradually reshaping the gaming landscape. More and more games like CryptoKitties, Decentraland, and Axie Infinity are proof-of-concept that the integration of blockchain in gaming can create an entirely new genre of games, often referred to as blockchain games or crypto games.

These games not only set the stage for players to experience unfettered ownership of their assets but also promise exciting opportunities for developers and investors. We envision an ecosystem where developers can craft games leaving the door open for massive player involvement, empowering them with the ability to create and trade assets. On the other hand, investors can explore opportunities in digital real estates or rare assets and yield profits from their smart investments.

The marriage of video gaming with blockchain technology opens an entirely new frontier of possibilities and opportunities. As we venture into this gaming metamorphosis that blurs the traditional video gaming boundaries, it promises a more integrative, immersive, and economically rewarding gaming experience.

Chapter 10. The Future Prospects of Blockchain in Gaming: The Experts' Insight

In the last decade, the gaming industry has seen various technological interventions playing vital roles in its evolution. As we embark on a new decade, the limelight is now on blockchain technology taking center stage. This chapter provides an immersive exploration into the future prospects of blockchain in gaming, with expert insight on its potential, implications, and challenges.

10.1. The Evolution of Gaming: The Rise of Blockchain

The current generation of gamers no longer just want to play games. Gamers want to influence game development, monetize their skills, own their digital assets, and interact freely with the gaming community. Blockchain technology is the perfect solution to meet these modern needs. By fostering transparency, decentralization, and interoperability, blockchain offers a seamless platform where gamers can truly own and have control over their digital assets.

Blockchain technology can anchor an ecosystem in which game developers, gamers, and even spectators can engage with one another in a more immersive and meaningful way. It opens up a world where gamers can monetize their unique in-game items or abilities, creating a potentially substantial market for digital goods and services.

10.2. Digital Assets: The Role of Tokenization

Tokenization is one of the key aspects of blockchain that will have a significant impact on the gaming industry. The security of blockchain technology makes it possible for developers to create non-fungible tokens (NFTs), each representing exclusive in-game items. This uniqueness can lead to rare, collectible items that can be sold or traded, potentially increasing the value of in-game purchases.

Experts believe that blockchain and NFTs will lead to the rise of "play-to-earn" games. This type of game design will enable players to trade virtual goods and currencies for real money, creating an Enterprise Market. Consequently, this will provide gamers with new avenues for income generation while offering collectors new methods for investing in in-game art and assets.

10.3. Blockchain and Cryptocurrency: An Economic Mechanism

Blockchain and cryptocurrency have intertwined futures in gaming. Cryptocurrencies such as Bitcoin and Ethereum are already prevalent in many online games, where they are used as a medium of exchange. This not only provides gamers with a method to transact value within a game but also carry that value beyond the game itself, creating further economic possibilities.

Experts foresee a future where every game has its native cryptocurrency, leading to seamless in-game purchases and transactions between players.

Blockchain, with its inherent security and transparency, can help ensure fair and auditable transactions, thus ensuring the gamer's trust in the system.

10.4. Embracing Interoperability: Blockchain's Promise

One of blockchain's brightest prospects in gaming is the concept of interoperability. This feature will allow assets from one game to be used in other games, providing new levels of interactivity and immersion. Blockchain can give birth to virtual worlds where players can move their digital goods between completely different gaming ecosystems.

This interoperability carries profound implications. Developers can collaborate to create super-games lifted by the contributions of different gaming communities. This could potentially spark the creation of a 'Metaverse' – a collective virtual shared space that is imagined to be the next significant evolution in gaming.

10.5. The Challenges Ahead: Scalability, Education, and Regulation

While blockchain brings exciting prospects, it is not without challenges. Its scalability issues have been a stumbling block since its inception. Games with millions of daily active users can face latency issues due to the slow transaction times typical of many blockchains. Solutions like layer-two networks, sidechains, sharding, and improved consensus mechanisms are being researched to address this issue.

Apart from technical difficulties, the education of players and developers in understanding this new technology is a hurdle.

Demystifying blockchain and making it approachable is critical for its mainstream adoption in the gaming industry.

On the regulatory front, legal complexities associated with cryptocurrencies and tokenization have yet to be satisfactorily resolved. Lawmakers have been slow to catch up with the pace of technology, and this can pose a noteworthy barrier to the adoption of blockchain in gaming.

10.6. The Road Ahead: An Exciting Post-Blockchain Gaming Era

Despite the challenges, the future of blockchain in gaming looks promising. With its unique benefits of promoting transparency, ownership, and security of in-game digital assets, the adoption of blockchain in gaming could potentially change the landscape of the industry. This technology promises a future where game development is more community-driven, where gamers can monetize their skills, and where complex virtual economies thrive.

In broad conclusion, blockchain is not just a technical upgrade for games; it is a societal upgrade. By implementing this technology, we underpin a future where creativity is rewarded, property rights are respected, and the relationship between developers and gamers is radically transformed. The possibilities are endless as the gaming industry gears up to embrace its blockchain-powered future.

Chapter 11. Guidelines for Gamers and Developers: Navigating the Blockchain Gaming Ecosystem

The blockchain world seems like a technological labyrinth at first glance. It's a place full of jargon, complex ideas, and new concepts. But don't let that intimidate you. With the correct roadmap and compass, anyone can navigate these unfamiliar terrains with confidence. This guideline aims to navigate you, whether you're a gamer or developer, through the blockchain-driven gaming ecosystem.

11.1. The Blockchain Basics

Before progressing, it's crucial to comprehend the underlying basics of blockchain technology. In its simplest form, a blockchain is a digital ledger that can't be altered or destroyed once created - it's immutable. A new block is added to the blockchain every time a transaction or an operation is carried out: each block contains the transaction's data. All of these blocks are linked together, forming a chain.

Blockchain can greatly increase transparency and security. It's decentralized, which ensures that no single entity has full control or can manipulate it. This decentralization also means it's nearly impervious to cyber attacks.

11.2. Understanding Blockchain in Gaming

With an understanding of blockchain, let's delve into how it intertwines with gaming — a union which promises an entertaining yet secure gaming experience.

In a blockchain-powered game, unique digital assets can be created, owned, and traded by players. These digital assets or "tokens" exist on the blockchain, making ownership transparent and secure. They enable players to have complete ownership of their in-game items, and even profit from them. Blockchain also ensures fairness and transparency in multiplayer or competitive games by ensuring that all actions are recorded and can't be tampered with.

11.3. Gamers' Guide to Blockchain Gaming

For gamers, the allure of blockchain gaming lies in the concept of "play-to-earn." Players have the chance to earn real-world value through their in-game actions.

Here are a few tips to ease into blockchain gaming:

1. Understand the Game Economy: Take the time to deeply understand a game's economy before diving in.

2. Know Your Tokens: Tokens can represent in-game assets or currency. Familiarize yourself with these before playing.

3. Secure Your Assets: Using a secure wallet to store your game tokens is vital. Check reviews and ensure you choose one celebrated for its security features.

4. Dive into the Community: Every game has a thriving community. Connect with them to learn tips, strategies, and to stay updated

on game development.

11.4. Developers' Guide to Blockchain Gaming

For developers, blockchain opens up innovative ways to engage with and reward their players. It also opens up a new revenue stream through the creation and selling of unique digital assets.

As a developer, moving into blockchain gaming requires a paradigm shift. Traditional concepts of game economy, player rewards, and even game design might need to be reevaluated.

1. Redefining Game Economy: The opportunity for players to earn or own assets changes the game economy. Make sure your designs take this element into account.

2. Familiarity with Smart Contracts: In-game mechanics could be run with Smart Contracts. Your team will need to learn how to use them.

3. Ensure a Sustainable Ecosystem: Unlike traditional games, players will be continuously earning in your game environment. Guarantee that this revenue model is sustainable.

4. Compliance and Regulation: As blockchain ties in with real-world value, ensure that your game complies with relevant legal and financial regulations.

11.5. The Future of Blockchain Gaming

Immersive, secure, and profitable – the benefits of blockchain gaming are too many to ignore. As the technology matures and blockchain games begin to approach the quality of traditional games, the future looks vibrant. For gamers and developers alike, the intersection of blockchain and gaming is a frontier worth exploring. And with this guide, you're well-prepared to take the first step into this brave new world.

In conclusion, the amalgamation of blockchain technology and the gaming industry is revolutionizing the way we perceive, play, and create games. The navigation through this transformative ecosystem may seem daunting, but the potential rewards — for gamers, developers, and the industry at large — are breathtaking to contemplate. As we move forward into this compelling future, this guide will serve as your roadmap. So gear up, and step into a new horizon of boundless possibilities and thrilling challenges. The blockchain gaming revolution has just begun.

www.ingramcontent.com/pod-product-compliance
Lightning Source LLC
Chambersburg PA
CBHW071015260726
48661CB00007B/2976